Binx Lost in France

By Michelle Hird

TINY TREE
CHILDREN'S BOOKS

First Published 2019
Tiny Tree Children's Books (an imprint of Matthew James Publishing Ltd)
Unit 46, Goyt Mill
Marple
Stockport
SK6 7HX

www.tinytreebooks.com

ISBN: 978-1-910265-79-6

Reprinted in 2022

© Michelle Hird
The moral rights of the author(s) have been asserted.

Apart from any fair dealing for the purpose of research, or private study, or criticism or review as permitted under the Copyright, Designs and Patents Act, 1988, this publication may only be reproduced, stored or transmitted in any form, or by any means, with the prior permission of the publisher, or in the case of reprographic reproduction, in accordance with the terms of licenses issued by the Copyright Licensing Agency. Enquiries concerning reproduction outside those terms should be sent to the publisher.

Binx and his family booked a trip to France,
he was so excited that he could sing and dance.

Two weeks later they took the train, even in his cat box he didn't complain.

Exploring the city, ever so happily, so much so, he lost his family.

He looked to his left, he looked to his right,
no matter where he looked, they were nowhere in sight.

Binx ran off quickly to pick up a trace,
feeling overwhelmed, he slowed his pace.

It suddenly dawned on him, he was **LOST!**
How would he get home? How much would it cost?

"I'll take you to your family. Come with me."

"Really, are you sure?!"

Binx said with glee!

Suddenly ... Binx remembered what he had been taught,
WHO to speak to, WHERE to go and WHAT to do, he thought.
Just because strangers don't have sharp teeth and red eyes,
they can still do us harm and tell us lies.

The stranger sensed that Binx was scared,
"Come with me, I've got sweets" he declared.
With the three Ws in his mind,
Binx shouted **"NO!"** then ran away, leaving the stranger behind.

Then, he spotted something that gave him hope,
dashing over to a mum and a child, he gave her a poke.

Binx's eyes were flooding with frustration,
The mother knew what to do and took him to the police station.

He could tell she was caring and meant him no harm,
walking alongside them, he was feeling more calm.

People at the station spoke a language unknown,
he wished he was with his family, curled up at home.

WAIT! ... his collar contained his telephone and address, he pointed to it quickly, hoping to put an end to this mess!

The call was made and Binx's family arrived,
so thrilled to see them, that he cried and he cried.
Binx was lucky that he was not harmed by this stranger,
he learnt a valuable lesson: some are a danger.
Knowing your numbers, addresses and names are a must,
always remember, there are strangers you can and can't trust.
You should never leave and go off on your own.
Follow your family, even when you're away from home.

The main thing you should do
is to keep yourself safe,
If you get lost remember these rules
and have some faith.

Dedicated to my family;
my Mum, my Dad and my two Sisters.
I would be lost without you.